HONORING GRIEF

Creating a Space to Let Yourself Heal

ALEXANDRA KENNEDY, MA

New Harbinger Publications, Inc.

Publisher's Note

This publication is designed to provide accurate and authoritative information in regard to the subject matter covered. It is sold with the understanding that the publisher is not engaged in rendering psychological, financial, legal, or other professional services. If expert assistance or counseling is needed, the services of a competent professional should be sought.

Distributed in Canada by Raincoast Books

Copyright © 2014 by Alexandra Kennedy
New Harbinger Publications, Inc.
5674 Shattuck Avenue
Oakland, CA 94609
www.newharbinger.com

Cover design by Amy Shoup;
Text design by Michele Waters-Kermes;
Acquired by Jess O'Brien;
Edited by Jennifer Eastman

Library of Congress Cataloging-in-Publication Data

Kennedy, Alexandra.
  Honoring grief : creating a space to let yourself heal / Alexandra Kennedy ; foreword by Stephen Levine.
      pages cm
  ISBN 978-1-62625-064-2 (paperback) -- ISBN 978-1-62625-065-9 (pdf e-book) -- ISBN 978-1-62625-066-6 (epub) 1. Grief. 2. Loss (Psychology) I. Title.
  BF575.G7K4577 2014
  155.9'3--dc23

                    2014021290

Printed in the United States of America

17   16   15

10   9   8   7   6   5   4   3   2

"This is a gentle, quiet book. Alexandra Kennedy [
pathways; authentic, genuine, heart-shredding grief is a fiercely intimate, intensely private matter, experienced in vastly unpredictable
ways. We are thrust against our will into some brand new world,
unique for each and every one of us. While she offers gentle suggestions, simple tools, and practices along the way, Kennedy wisely coun-
sels there is 'no map, no schedule.' There is tremendous mercy here.
We are too often rushed through what must be allowed its time, its
season, to ripen, to die, to heal.

"Kennedy is wise and compassionate, and she refuses to desecrate this
holy mystery of loss. Rather, she offers simply to accompany us as we
walk a path only we can follow. Kennedy teaches us to trust that Death
knows the way to lead us into Life. For us, we can trust that Kennedy
knows of what she speaks."

> **—Wayne Muller**, author of *Sabbath* and *A Life of Being,*
> *Having, and Doing Enough*

"A true pioneer in our field, Alexandra Kennedy offers a profoundly
clear understanding of what it truly means to heal after a loss in her
elegantly simple new book, *Honoring Grief*. It's sure to become a classic.
For years to come, I'll be sharing this wonderful book with clients,
families, friends, and communities besieged by loss."

> **—Ken Druck, PhD**, grief and resilience coach and
> author of *The Real Rules of Life: Balancing Life's Terms*
> *with Your Own*

"If there is one person I'd like to talk to after a loss, it is Alexandra
Kennedy. She offers no platitudes for grief—no one-size-fits-all
recipe—just wisdom, kindness, and empathy. Most of all, Kennedy
tells us what we all need to hear: we are not alone, and, no, we are not
going crazy."

> **—Lolly Winston, MFA**, author of the novels *Good*
> *Grief* and *Happiness Sold Separately*

"We don't usually think of grief as a healing journey; in fact, most of us would rather not think of grief at all. But Alexandra Kennedy gently, expertly guides the reader into a depth that is neither frightening nor overwhelming, but manageable and critical to one's true well-being. In *Honoring Grief*, she has distilled a lifetime of listening and examining to bring forth a sacred practice that allows us to meet grief where we are, be embraced in sanctuary, heal wounds, and renew life with new eyes and a more open heart. With this book's practices, grief can be a time to break free from the pain of long-held sufferings, and expand our capacity to love and live fully."

> **—Beth Witrogen**, Pulitzer Prize nominee and author of *Caregiving: The Spiritual Journey of Love, Loss, and Renewal*

"Grief is the way that loss heals. In *Honoring Grief*, Alexandra Kennedy offers us a sanctuary in which to process our losses and find healing. This simple-to-use, step-by-step workbook on the healing of grief can be a nightlight for people in dark times."

> **—Rachel Naomi Remen, MD**, author of *Kitchen Table Wisdom* and *My Grandfather's Blessings*

"I loved this book. *Honoring Grief* provides safety, comfort, and guidance for healing after loss. The format makes it easily accessible to someone experiencing deep chaotic emotions. The text is poetic and beautifully crafted. I would recommend this book to my colleagues and friends. It will become part of my teaching."

> **—Janet M. Schreiber, PhD**, director of the Grief, Loss, and Trauma certificate program at Southwestern College, Santa Fe, New Mexico

For my son, Taylor,
who lights up my life

Contents

Foreword

Grief is love. Grief is a great shock, but no surprise. We have momentarily imagined the loss of loved ones and instinctively pushed such fleeting thoughts aside. But now it is our dear loved ones who look back beseechingly, asking us to forgive ourselves, love ourselves, remember those still at our side.

In the heart swollen with grief there is room for only a few words that remind us of the divinity of love and the kindness it breeds. Alexandra offers these finely wrought (on the hard anvil of need, with the soft-tipped brush of the heart) words to heal what can never be broken.

—Stephen Levine

Introduction

Grief touches us all. At different times of our lives, it finds each one of us—and we are often unprepared for its intensity and hesitant to plunge into its transformative depth. You may be holding this book in your hands because there was a major loss that has hit you in the past year—the death of a loved one or the loss of a relationship, your health, or a job. Or, worried about a grieving family member or friend, you may be looking for resources to understand and support him or her. There may be small losses that have accumulated in the flurry of everyday life; perhaps some recent loss has triggered an old, buried grief that needs healing now. Or it is time to begin the process of healing generational grief—an unresolved loss that has been passed down to you from your parents, grandparents, or even great-grandparents.

Ungrieved losses take a toll on our hearts and deaden us to life. When we are fully alive, we embrace the joys and sorrows inherent in life; when there is a loss, we grieve. A heart transformed by grief is capable of giving and receiving genuine love and of feeling compassion for our fellow human beings.

How then can we grieve in the midst of our daily lives? How can we tap the power of grief to transform our lives, open our hearts, and awaken us to a deeper participation in the world? On this healing journey, we want guidance and inspiration; we want to understand how we can get through the pain. We want to know we will heal. This is why we turn to books about grief. The irony is that when we are grieving, we don't have the energy, patience, or inclination to read books—especially ones with a lot of text or concepts. A page full of words can feel daunting; sometimes we can read only a couple sentences at a time. How then can a book inspire and guide those who are grieving without overwhelming them?

The format of *Honoring Grief* has been created with this in mind. There are just a few thoughts per page; these carefully chosen words offer a distilled wisdom that has come from my years of teaching and clinical practice as a psychotherapist. The short bursts of forthright, poetic language allow you, the reader, to project your own experiences and imagination onto the book and to take in suggestions and insights about grief with space to integrate all this into your daily life.

This book offers unique strategies and opportunities for healing as you explore the sacred territory of grief. I invite you to read slowly—perhaps just a page or sentence at a time. You may find that you read certain pages over and over, with something new gleaned each time. Explore the exercises. Linger over what you've read. Soak it in. See how you respond. Reflect on what it brings up for you emotionally. Notice what resonates. Honor your own unique experience and expression of grief.

If you are newly encountering grief, part 1 shows you how grief works and what to expect while you are grieving. You'll also learn how people often avoid their grief, along with symptoms of unresolved grief. If you are further along in your grieving, you will be able to review what is a normal part of the grieving process; you'll be encouraged not to pull yourself out of grief prematurely.

Part 2 introduces the powerful concept of the sanctuary, which I developed while grieving the loss of my father (you can read more about this in my book *Losing a Parent*) and refined over the past two decades in my psychotherapy practice, teaching, and writing. This strategy involves creating a specific place in our homes dedicated to our healing—and then spending a limited time there daily. The sanctuary is a sacred space that gently holds us as we turn within; it becomes a crucible of healing when chaotic feelings are activated in grief. After years of using the sanctuary myself, working with clients and students, and corresponding with readers of my two books on grief, I understand better the dynamics that make this seemingly simple strategy so successful for healing grief. The sanctuary has consistently made the biggest difference in the progress of therapy for my clients, even in cases of complicated grief. It has become a cornerstone of my work, not only for grieving clients, but also for those who are going through life transitions and challenges.

For those of you who have regrets or unresolved issues with a deceased loved one, part 3 explores how it is never too late to reconcile and heal your relationship. You'll learn how to nurture the ongoing inner relationship with a deceased loved one. The relationship we have continues to change—so it is important not to let memories and old images dictate the nature of the relationship after death.

The final part of *Honoring Grief* offers stimulating ideas for recreating your life after a significant loss. You will explore the greatest grief we often carry—for ourselves, for the unlived moments, for all the times we have not lived true to ourselves.

As you embrace your grief with awareness, with kindness, and with enough depth to heal, you may find that you feel lighter and more at peace in your heart. With a heart that is flexible, fluid, and open to the world, you can more fully embrace this precious life—with all its mystery, beauty, joys, and sorrows.

May you find healing, comfort, and inspiration in these pages.

May you learn to trust grief and let it take you where you need to go to heal.

May your heart heal of old wounds and regrets so that it may open to greater love and joy.

May you celebrate—every day—the wonder and mystery of being fully alive.

PART 1

The Nature of Grief: What We Can Expect

Over a lifetime, we will experience many losses. Growing up, we lose friends, pets, possessions, houses, grandparents, teachers, sometimes parents. By middle age, the losses mount up—the loss of youth, loved ones, unfulfilled dreams, health, homes, careers, and jobs. Our children leave home; some of us feel the loss of never having had children. Many lose partners or spouses to divorce or death—or emotional distance. By old age, we are faced with letting go of everything we once held dear.

When we are fully alive, we embrace both our joys and sorrows. When something delights us, we celebrate; when we experience a loss, we grieve.

We live by losing, leaving, and letting go;
as with the seasons, we go through cycles
of release and renewal. Each one of us will
be called on at different times in our lives
to face loss. Will we embrace it or shrink
from it?

Most of us naturally shrink from loss.
We think that we can avoid loss if we keep
busy or close our hearts a little to protect
ourselves. Our losses accumulate—unfelt,
unacknowledged, unresolved.

Ungrieved losses take a toll on our hearts.
We shut down—from life, from one another,
from ourselves. The grief remains buried
in the psyche and body; it affects our
relationships and compromises our aliveness.

At some later time, sometimes when we least
expect it, the grief erupts. Many of us have
current problems rooted in the death or loss
of a loved one that was never grieved. Almost
all of us carry some degree of unresolved,
unhealed grief that congests our hearts.

Unresolved grief can show up in such symptoms as

chronic physical ailments,

fearfulness,

depression,

overworking,

addiction,

social isolation,

compulsive behavior.

We pay a deep price for our unresolved grief; however, no matter how many years have passed, we can tap into a wise, intelligent force of healing that is available within each one of us.

Rather than resist the powerful, transformative forces activated in grief, we can learn strategies for moving through it—or more accurately, allowing it to move through us, stage by stage, day by day—without feeling overwhelmed. Once we let down into grief and let it move through us (without blocking its flow), it shows us what we need to heal.

Reflect on the losses you have experienced in your life up to now. Create a timeline of your life from birth to the present and mark on it all the losses you have experienced—include how old you were at each loss and the feelings that the loss generated. Include all kinds of losses—the loss of family members, lovers, friends, pets, homes, security, neighborhoods, teachers, precious possessions, health, money, dreams, and all others.

Opening to the little losses will make room for the bigger ones when they come along.

Beneath your timeline, write some notes about

> what your parents taught you about grief and loss,
>
> how they dealt with their own losses,
>
> how they expected you to act when you had a significant loss,
>
> how you've dealt with old losses.

Go back now and circle all the losses on your timeline that were never actively grieved or perhaps were never even acknowledged. When you think about them now, these old losses might trigger feelings—feelings that are still painful even though years, not days, have passed. If you thought it would just take time to heal your grief, you will be surprised.

Each of us carries a well of grief that holds
    the ungrieved losses of a lifetime,
    places in us that have not known love,
    grief handed down through generations,
    the shared, collective sense of human
      sorrow.

We might not recognize this deep
undercurrent of loss until we lose a loved one.

As we inhabit our depths and heal our grief, we gain access to a source of soul-nourishing waters—waves of prayer, inspiration, and love all flow from this source.

When we experience a loss, it is common for the mind to try to find a way out of the pain. We go over and over what we could have said or done; we repeatedly review details of our last time together. This can lead to obsessive thinking, anxiety, and insomnia. We will not heal our grief if we stay at this mental level. We cannot think our way out of grief.

In grief, we learn to cherish what is truly important.

Many of us carry beliefs about grieving:

> Grief will heal in time by itself.
>
> I should be back to normal after six weeks.
>
> If I am strong and stay busy, I will get through the grief without any repercussions.
>
> If I start crying, I will never stop.
>
> If I really heal and let go, I will lose my loved one forever.

What are your strongly held beliefs around grief?

    1.

    2.

    3.

These beliefs can lead to postponing or ignoring grief, but in so doing, they seriously compromise our capacity for aliveness. They can block the natural flow of healing that occurs after a loss.

As you turn toward your grief, what would it be like to grieve without the old concepts and fears? As you enter into relationship with this wise, healing force within you, what will you discover?

Grief can surprise you with its power, its unpredictable timing, its fathomless depth, its transformational potential, and the scope of change it brings into your life.

We discover that grief has its own nature, rhythm, and timing; it resists our attempts to control it. We also discover that grief involves more ongoing changes in our lives than we could have ever imagined. It reaches into every part of our lives—our family, relationships, work, health, sleep, emotions, and sense of identity. No part of our lives is left untouched.

Grief is slow. It takes time. It goes deep.

There is no map, no schedule.

If we do not interfere with or resist the natural flow of grief, how might it work in us? Grief turns us inward and downward. It takes us out of our heads, into our hearts and bellies, into our depths.

Feelings come in waves, arising out of our depths and bowling us over with their intensity. There are periods of calm, even peace. Conflicting feelings can arise simultaneously. We never know what to expect.

Grief
    peels away masks,
    breaks the mind's habits,
    slows us down,
    takes us deep inside ourselves,
    rearranges our insides,
    churns up unresolved issues,
    brings everything into question.

This is how grief transforms us.

Grief brings us to our knees. It is humbling to realize that grief is so much more powerful than we are. We realize how fragile we are, how precious life is, how our lives can change in an instant. We will never return to the life we knew before the loss of a loved one. We will never be the same.

Few experiences have the power that grief does—to humble, transform, and expand us.

PART 2

Creating a Sanctuary
for Grieving

Grief is wise. It knows what you need to feel whole again.

We can deepen into grief without feeling overwhelmed.

We can learn to actively grieve and still attend to our daily lives.

We can heal our regrets.

The sanctuary is a powerful yet simple strategy for healing our grief without feeling overwhelmed. We create a sacred space that gently holds us as we turn within; it sustains us as we move through the stages of grief. It enables us to honor our grief for a limited time each day in the midst of our busy lives. Rather than feeling overwhelmed, those who use the sanctuary find that they have much more focus and energy for their work, schoolwork, friends, and families.

Why is the sanctuary so effective? What makes it so transformative?

- It creates a safe, insulated, contained space. This container holds and builds the energy necessary for transformation and healing in the psyche.

- It is time limited. Many people are willing to embrace uncomfortable states of being (such as grief) when there is a clear time limit.

- It allows us to go deep enough to heal.

- The sanctuary is empowering to use—
  any one, including children, can use it.
  Those who use it discover that once
  frightening or troubling emotional
  states of grief can be embraced more
  effectively in small bits.

- Using the sanctuary regularly generates
  a sense of peace in the midst of
  grieving. This provides the incentive
  to use it daily.

Be creative, thoughtful, and daring in creating your sanctuary. Let it be a place that inspires, comforts, and nurtures you in your grief. Find a contained space in your home or garden where you feel protected and safe. It's important that you will not be interrupted. Removed from the demands and distractions of your daily life, the sanctuary is a refuge dedicated to your healing.

If you find that you don't feel at ease in a location, move the sanctuary to another place. Most people need to try out different places until they settle on one that works. For example, you might not feel comfortable in a small, enclosed room; you might choose instead a sheltered corner of your garden as a sanctuary.

After finding the place for your sanctuary, create a specific area that you can focus on when you sit in the sanctuary. Think of this as a small personal altar that honors your grief. Arrange pictures, flowers, stones, shells, jewelry, candles, pieces of fabric, bowls, small statues, or whatever you feel connects you to your loss. Feel free to rearrange your altar regularly; you might find that what you want in your sanctuary changes as you move through your grief.

Set a regular time for using the sanctuary daily. Experiment with this until you find a time of the day that works best for you. The important thing is to use it daily—so that there is a rhythm of turning within, then returning to your daily life. If you feel anxious about using the sanctuary, start with ten minutes or less. As you feel more confident, gradually increase the time, building up to twenty or thirty minutes.

Shorter, more focused times in the sanctuary seem to work better than longer periods, which might overwhelm you emotionally. The key is to turn your attention within and deepen into whatever is taking place inside you during that session. It is the depth we access when we grieve that heals the psyche—not the length of time in the sanctuary.

As you enter the sanctuary each day, make sure that you won't be disturbed. Put a note on your door; turn off the phone. You are now entering a sacred space of grieving. Think of the sanctuary as a cocoon that holds and protects you while you are in a vulnerable state of transformation and change—much as the cocoon protects the caterpillar as it transforms into the butterfly.

Sit down. Take a couple of deep breaths, softn your belly, and settle into your sanctuary. Take a few minutes to let your eyes pass over pictures and objects you have placed on your altar. As your eyes linger there, let the reality sink in that your loss has indeed occurred; it takes time to fully absorb this.

Grief resides in your heart and belly; if you want to heal, gently let your attention drop into your body.

Close your eyes and turn your attention within. What is happening inside you? What most wants your attention? Scan your body. Our bodies are in a constant conversation with us; our bodies don't lie—though our minds do. Without changing anything, what are you experiencing in your body right now? What sensations come to your attention? Which areas are holding tension? Where is grief residing in your body?

As you tune in to your body, be aware of your emotions. Grief brings up a wide range of feelings, which can change quickly and sometimes seem to conflict with one another. Are you feeling sad? Angry? Relieved? Numb? Guilty? Lost? Depressed? Peaceful? Embrace any feelings you are experiencing just as they are, without trying to change or understand them. Your priority is to simply feel them.

The sanctuary invites you to simply be yourself, just as you are in this moment. This is your time to check in with yourself—without editing or judging—to be with whatever is going on within you. How you hold what comes up in the sanctuary is critically important for the healing process. If you judge a feeling as heavy or negative (or if you judge yourself for having a particular feeling), you are interfering with the flow of grief.

Feel whatever presents itself, without trying to change it, without bringing a story to it—everything is welcome. This is the key to healing.

After the check-in period, you can deepen into any issue that has come up. If you have unresolved issues with a loved one you have lost to death, divorce, or emotional distance, this would be a good time to explore them. Everything that shows up in the sanctuary is there for you to experience fully in that moment as part of this healing journey. Don't escape; feel.

As we let down into whatever feelings or sensations we are having in this moment, we invite grief to flow through us without hindrance. We entrust ourselves to the waves of grief. We stop running from and arguing with the way life is. We stop trying to change ourselves.

In the safe refuge of the sanctuary, absorb the impact of how your world has changed, both within and without. Sit in the silence of the sanctuary without knowing what will happen. Open your heart to discovery, to mystery, to the unknown. You are learning to flow with this grieving process.

It's a revolutionary moment when you realize that nothing else needs to happen—all you need to "do" is to trust how life (and your grief) is unfolding in this moment. It's as though you tell yourself, *I'll be here with you, however you are in this moment.* What a relief to rest as you are! To meet yourself fully in the sanctuary is an act of love.

Cradle yourself in your sorrow; be
gentle with yourself.

It is this capacity to go deep into the grief for a short period each day that builds confidence in our grieving. Each time we use the sanctuary, we get the nourishment and strength to go further in the process. We learn how to gracefully integrate our experience of loss into our daily lives.

A journal can be a good companion in your sanctuary. Keep one near so you can write when inspired. After your sanctuary check-in, you might want to write about what you just observed—the feelings, sensations, and thoughts that come to the foreground as you turn within. This is a good time to also explore and deepen into any issues that have come up. Record any dreams from the night before.

As you come to the end of your time in the sanctuary, write a few lines about your experience there that day. Review your journal from time to time, so you can see the progress of your healing and follow the thread of certain themes over time. When the time you've allotted for your active grieving has passed, remind yourself that you will have sanctuary time again tomorrow. Then get up and leave the sanctuary.

When you leave the sanctuary, let go of focusing on the grief. Make a clear transition. Many people hold on to their grief. It is important to grieve fully in the sanctuary but to let go of it when it is time to engage in your daily life. To help with the transition, do something nurturing for yourself—have a cup of tea, call a friend, go for a walk.

Immerse yourself in nature. There is so much soul nourishment in the patience of trees, the quiet strength of stones, and the comforting ebb and flow of tides at the ocean's edge. The earth continually reminds us that we are part of an eternal, universal rhythm; the light returns faithfully after the darkest night, and the green explosion of spring follows even the bleakest winter.

It is not unusual to experience at least some resistance to using the sanctuary, even when you feel excited about the prospect of the healing that can come from it. It is normal to resist facing pain and intense feelings. Acknowledge this resistance; don't ignore or fight it.

Name your fears; make a list of them.

For example, I'm afraid of

    losing control,

    crying so hard that I can't stop,

    being overwhelmed,

    falling into a bottomless pit,

    becoming nonfunctional,

    becoming paralyzed with the pain,

    losing control, or

    being left alone.

It is possible to be aware of our fears of grieving and simultaneously explore the sanctuary as a strategy for healing and transformation. If you are feeling resistant to using the sanctuary, shorten your time there but show up every day for a week or two. Then compare how you feel each day as you leave the sanctuary with how you felt before you started using it. Approach the sanctuary as an experiment.

If you are dealing with multiple losses, the fear of being overwhelmed is magnified. Dedicate each session in the sanctuary to one loss. Put out pictures and objects related to the loss you are focusing on that day. Stay with each loss for as long as it takes to feel some inner shift or healing. Then turn to the next loss.

As healing progresses, you may need to use the sanctuary less frequently, but you should still use it from time to time to check in. This keeps you honest with your grief. Inevitably, you will find that the sanctuary yields a very different experience from what you feared you would have. You may discover that you don't feel overwhelmed by the feelings that surface. You may begin to experience your time in the sanctuary as a homecoming.

It is important to actively work to integrate and heal your grief, rather than just passively experience your reactions to it. There are tasks in grieving, and the sanctuary is a good place to focus on these tasks. Every so often, consider a review of the seven tasks of grieving described in the next two pages. In different sanctuary sessions, are you devoting some attention to each of these tasks?

Seven Tasks of Grieving the Loss of a Loved One

- Experience and express all the feelings over your loss.

- Let the nonnegotiable and excruciating reality sink in that you will never again be in the physical presence of your loved one.

- Review your relationship from the beginning and see both the positive and negative aspects of the person and the relationship.

- Identify and address your unresolved issues and regrets.

- Explore the changes in your family and other relationships.

- Nurture an inner relationship with your loved one and use your imagination to tap opportunities for healing, resolution, and guidance.

- Integrate all these changes into a new sense of yourself and take on healthy ways of being in the world without this person.

It is reassuring that you can go deep enough to heal—without feeling overwhelmed—and then leave the sanctuary with revitalized energy to deal with the demands of your daily life. As you leave a sanctuary session feeling more alive, vital, and peaceful, you may begin to see a big difference in the quality of your day when you use the sanctuary compared with those days when you don't.

Grief opens us inward to new depths—
but also outward to new vistas.

Integrate your loss into your community of family and friends. Relationships often change. You may find that you need more depth and authenticity in your relationships. Unexpected people might show up to give you support, while others you had counted on might withdraw, probably out of their own discomfort with grief.

Seek out others who can support you in your grief by providing safe witness and listening

without judging,

without trying to fix you,

without giving you advice,

without minimizing your experience.

When you give voice to your sorrow (with someone who can respectfully hold the space for you), you share your humanity—and with it, the connectedness of all human suffering.

The sanctuary invites us to be just as we are in our grief. This is its biggest gift. What healing is generated when life can flow through us without resistance! Usually we screen out what we don't want to see or feel in ourselves. However, whatever we repress robs us of energy and compromises our capacity for aliveness. What a shift it is to open to whatever is right here—in our bodies, our feelings, our thoughts—and to turn toward whatever rises in our experience.

It's a relief to not try to be anyone else or anywhere else, to allow ourselves to be exactly as we are, without judging ourselves. When we are able to meet ourselves in this way, we naturally feel at home in ourselves. We rest in being; we relax and begin to feel comfortable in our own skin. In the midst of our grieving, we feel present and whole—no longer divided.

In grief, you gather your heart back to yourself again.

PART 3

Healing Old Hurts,
Saying Good-Bye,
Expressing Love

After the loss of a loved one, many of us are left with old hurts unhealed, good-byes unsaid, love unexpressed. We grieve not only the person but also the hopes, dreams, and unfulfilled expectations that we had for and with that person. Our unfinished business can keep us from letting go and going on with our lives. These wounds can taint all our relationships.

You have the power within yourself to create
and recreate your relationships, to heal old
wounds, to experience deep intimacy. Your
beloved is within reach—within you—much
closer than you think. All that is keeping
you from a sense of connection with your
deceased loved one is your unused
imagination. In the imagination, death
does not end a relationship.

It is never too late to reconcile and heal your relationship with a deceased loved one.

It is in dreams that many have the first experience of their ongoing inner relationship with a deceased loved one. As you awaken from a dream about your loved one, you may think, *She's still alive!* and then realize your loved one has died.

Our dreams seem to offer us the message that both are true: your loved one has died in the physical realm, but he or she is still alive within you.

Dreams arise from the unconscious and communicate important information about how grief is affecting us at this deep level of the psyche. Offering invaluable guidance, they guide our work in the sanctuary as they confirm recent breakthroughs, alert us to what we are rejecting, and point out what we need to address in order to heal.

If we approach dreams with respect, humility, and receptivity, we will build a constructive working relationship with the unconscious. We will remember more and more dreams; dreams will become more vivid and instructive.

In training yourself to remember your dreams, the first step is to place a pad of paper, pen, and flashlight by your bed. Go to sleep with the intention of remembering your dreams, along with the willingness to listen to their messages.

When you awaken in the morning, rest awhile in the threshold state between sleep and waking. Don't talk or move out of bed until you have recorded your dreams. If you awaken from a dream in the middle of the night, record it before going back to sleep (as much as the conscious mind insists that you will remember the dream in the morning, you most likely won't).

Start with brief notes that sketch out the dream (a few key words, not even sentences). Later that day you can record the dream in more detail in your journal. Don't edit as you write it down. An ordinary detail in the dream that you think is inconsequential may be much more significant than you realize. Write out the dream in the present tense, as though it is happening right now. Give the dream a name.

An unexplored dream is like gold
cast away.

Sit with the dream in your sanctuary. Hold the images softly in your awareness. Images that arise freshly from the unconscious in dreams have considerable power to heal and alter your consciousness—even without your understanding what they mean. Let the images work on you; feel their power. Let them come alive, without interpreting them. Approach the dream humbly, setting aside snap judgments. You may feel baffled or disturbed by the dream, which is natural when working with dreams.

college

You can paint, draw, or sculpt the dream; dialogue with dream figures; act out the dream; or close your eyes and reenter the dream in order to explore one aspect more fully. Many people are shocked by how differently the deceased may appear in dreams—often they are younger, healthier, even happier and more open than they were in life. It's as though the dream is reminding us that the relationship has changed.

Don't let old memories dictate the nature of the relationship with a deceased loved one; be open to new possibilities.

Take advantage of the freedoms that the imagination provides

to break out of old patterns of relating,

to speak your truth,

to restore a lost dialogue,

to express your love,

to step inside another,

to transform an absence into a presence.

Some possibilities to explore in your sanctuary:

> Talk to your deceased loved one out loud or silently.
>
> Write a letter.
>
> Write a dialogue.
>
> Close your eyes and imagine meeting your loved one in a special place.

Writing a letter to a deceased loved one gives you the freedom to express whatever you have held back or silenced in a relationship. Of course, your letter will never be sent or read by the other person. The letter provides a safe place to unburden your heart—and the sanctuary is a safe place to write it.

You can start your letter in one session and continue it in subsequent sessions. Or you can complete a letter in one session. Express yourself fully, without editing your thoughts or feelings. Just allow what is stored inside to come out on the paper.

What do you regret? Appreciate? Resent? Miss?

What have you held back?

What issues have come between you?

What do you want to carry on?

What are you ready to let go of?

What did you learn from this relationship?

What promises did you make to this person?

Is it time to reevaluate these promises?

At first, letters may be full of anger. Don't be concerned about this. You may need to express uncomfortable feelings and thoughts before you can move on to feelings that are more loving or compassionate. Try to avoid blaming or preaching. The purpose is not to find fault with the other person; it is to express what is unresolved in your heart.

As you dive into your grief, you may at first encounter anger. Going deeper, you may discover a reservoir of sadness—and under that, a vast sea of love.

If unresolved issues call for a deeper communication or understanding, you can explore writing a dialogue with your loved one. Start with a question and then—without letting your mind get in the way—write an answer. Stay with this rhythm of question/ answer, question/answer until the flow of a dialogue begins to unfold.

As you reread your letter or dialogue, you might be surprised by the insights that emerge. It takes courage to suspend our normal mode of thinking and relax into the flow of communication and insight that comes from within. Be willing to let go and see what emerges and what rings true.

When you have finished writing for that day, read your letter. Feel where it has taken you in terms of healing.

Did you express yourself freely, honestly, and fully?

Did you address unresolved issues?

Do you still have regrets?

Did you express your love?

Do you feel forgiveness, compassion, or tenderness?

Another way of connecting with a deceased loved one is through imagery. Close your eyes and imagine a rose. Bring all your inner senses to this experience—see the rose, feel it, smell it. The petals of this rose are beginning to peel back, one at a time, to reveal its center—and at its center stands your loved one waiting for you.

Go to meet your loved one there and allow for your interaction to unfold, without editing. You may want to hold your loved one in your arms, talk, or just be together. When you are ready, let your loved one know that you will be visiting again and step out of the rose's center and watch the petals fold up again. Open your eyes and take some time to integrate what you have just experienced.

You can also imagine a special place where you meet your loved one. For example, close your eyes and imagine an open field, bringing all your inner senses to experiencing everything about this place. What do you see, hear, and smell in this place? From far away, you see a figure approaching and realize this is your loved one. Take some time to fully take in the presence of this person. See what unfolds as you come together.

After repeated experiences of connecting with your loved one through the imagination, your heart will acknowledge a comforting, affirming presence abiding within—a presence you now trust to be accessible whenever summoned. Let your relationship with your loved one continue to unfold—with or without words, by simply being together in your heart space.

To the imagination, death is not an ending; love is never lost.

As you heal from a significant loss, further grief may come up behind it. Tears may erupt seemingly out of nowhere; your heart may ache; dreams may emerge that don't make any sense in the context of your own life. This may be a collective grief that you are experiencing, or it could be a grief passed down through several generations that is now asking to be healed through you.

Perhaps, before you were born, your mother or grandmother lost a child whom she never fully grieved; perhaps your family in past generations experienced a significant loss or trauma that was never healed. When this generational grief surfaces, it is your work in the sanctuary to simply embrace the surge of feelings as they emerge, to pay attention to any images that come to mind, and to listen closely to your dreams for guidance.

Remember that every time you use the sanctuary, you can access the potent energies of healing and transformation that reside within grief. You can participate in this healing, but you can't control or force it. It will unfold at its own pace.

The deep wisdom of grief comes to us through a still, small voice from within, through gentle promptings and inspirations—if only we will listen. The sanctuary is a perfect environment for that listening. With our attention turned within, we are quiet, open, and receptive.

Some of the nudgings from this still, small
voice you might receive in your sanctuary are

to call a person,

to go to a place,

to read a passage in a book,

to reflect on a dream,

to listen to or sing a song,

to turn attention toward some unresolved
issue, some nagging regret.

When you stop resisting how grief works in you, you can learn what it wants to show you.

PART 4

Recreating Our
Lives after Loss

Grief changes us. We are no longer the person we were, nor are we the person we will be. Grief transforms our lives. We find that what was true about our lives is no longer true. Everything is different; we see with new eyes. What used to be important no longer matters to us. We walk on new, fertile ground.

Loss makes room for something new.

Grief clarifies what is important and what is not. It calls on you to recreate your life in a way that incorporates new perspectives, new priorities, and new values. After experiencing a significant loss, list what you now value most in your life.

1.

2.

3.

In the quiet of your sanctuary, you might find that questions begin to surface from the upheaval inherent in grief—the deep questions that invite you to look at the quality and authenticity of your life.

What brings me joy?

What is worth living for?

What do I want?

You may resist these questions at first; this is natural. It's not easy to reflect on our lives in this way. However, the process of questioning is one of the most creative aspects of the grieving process. It is these questions that will inspire you to look at what no longer sustains you, what is calling for your attention and energy, and where change is needed.

When questions about your life start to show up, embrace them without trying to come up with the answers. Let the questioning itself move you deeper into yourself. It is difficult to hold these questions in your consciousness without knowing where they are taking you; you naturally want to move away from that discomfort. Use the nurturing environment of the sanctuary to connect with your own knowing, your inherent wisdom.

Risk the release of old views; let your true heart speak.

If you let those questions work on you, your life will begin to open up in response—and gradually, answers may come. They could come in the silence of meditation, in a dream you had the night before, in a phrase you've just written in your journal or read in a book. Many times these answers are accompanied by a sense of knowing—a tingling or shudder that you can feel in your body—an "aha" moment.

Our lives are broken apart and recreated in times of grief.

Write out a list of questions that you've begun to turn over in your mind, or refer to the list of questions opposite and see if one grabs your attention. Let that question drop deep inside; allow it to move energy around in your body, to stir up emotions. Don't be concerned about the answers to the questions at this point; something much more significant is happening with the movement of energy and emotion.

Some questions to explore:

Am I living the life I really want?

What do I need to let go of in my life that is no longer alive?

What is sacred?

Who or what do I love?

What have I sacrificed in order to be successful?

What is calling to me now in my life?

How have I responded to or ignored that calling?

What changes would I need to make in order for my life to truly sustain me?

What new horizon in me wants to be seen?

Take one question at a time and sit quietly with it, turning it over, without thinking, without any pressure to come up with an answer. Be willing not to know. Or you can write about it in your journal. Each question may take a full session, part of a session, or several sessions in the sanctuary. What is important is that the questioning gets energy moving deep in the psyche. It is from here that change naturally unfolds.

Explore each question until the energy driving it is no longer there. As each question resolves in the heart (not necessarily by being answered), open to the spaciousness between the questions, between each thought— breathe into that spaciousness, relax into it. Let everything else drop away. This is the birthing place of galaxies, atoms, thoughts, new life. All possibilities emerge out of this emptiness.

Live your one and only life
to the fullest.

As you embrace life-changing questions, you will begin to see the need to integrate the shift in perspectives and values into every aspect of daily life—your relationships, family, work, sense of identity, community, body, goals, and creativity. Nothing is left untouched. Without realizing it at first, you may discover that you are indeed living the answers.

Some Suggestions for Recreating Your Life

- Notice which relationships or activities nourish you and which ones drain you. See who shows up for you as you are grieving and who doesn't; most people are surprised.

- Give yourself permission to withdraw from social activities or commitments that have been regular parts of your daily life. Wait to see what comes up to replace them.

- Find new ways to celebrate the holidays; create new family rituals.

- Experiment with expressing yourself in new ways through art, music, writing, and dance. Follow the muse when she pulls you to create—a decorated grief box, garden, collage, poem, or a special meal.

- Most of all, pay attention to where your energy is naturally drawn; don't discount a subtle yearning to do something different. Follow the energy; this is a glimpse of the new life that is unfolding.

Your grief will continue to flow through you; you will see its impact in every aspect of your life. Gradually you will be able to understand and integrate the suffering you have experienced. As grief invites you to be more intimate with your loved ones and with the earth, you will see how gratitude, compassion, and love are taking root in your life.

From time to time, a big wave of sorrow
might hit—sometimes out of the blue. It can
be disconcerting to feel such intense feelings
again. These waves are part of a long-term
healing process; they will continue to come
and go. Don't talk yourself out of this
experience; fully embrace the feelings
that surface.

The day will come when you realize it
is for yourself that you are grieving.

Loss by loss, we follow the trail back to ourselves. There we find that we are grieving

for all the unlived moments, for our unlived lives,

for the times we've not been true to ourselves,

for the ways we've compromised ourselves,

for what we've sacrificed to be successful or to win the approval of others.

Our grief wakes us up to life. We learn to bear the exquisite beauty and sorrow of being fully alive, to savor the simple moments, to cherish what's here now. If we can hold ourselves with compassion, we can hold others with compassion. If we can let ourselves be as we are, we can allow others to be as they are. We can begin to embrace life as it is in this moment and trust the flow of life as it unfolds. Then we learn to walk the earth with wonder.

Grieving is sacred work. It has the power to take you deep into your Source, where you will have a glimpse of your true home. That is where you find peace.

Acknowledgments

I will never forget the day I sketched out on paper the vision for this book; on my way home from our local coffee shop, I was greeted by a double rainbow that arched over the valley where my house is. With this brilliant blessing, I embarked on the long journey of birthing *Honoring Grief*. I am indebted to my friend Brian Erwin for his generosity in giving me valuable feedback on the proposal. Since *Honoring Grief* was to explore a new book format, graphic artist Kathleen Roberts mocked up some pages to show us what this book might look like—and it started to take tangible form. Many thanks to you both!

Gratitude to Jess O'Brien for writing me after he heard about my work on grieving at John F. Kennedy University—and for enthusiastically presenting *Honoring Grief* to his colleagues at New Harbinger Publications. In the book's development, the editorial staff at New Harbinger offered insightful suggestions and feedback. I quickly discovered that writing a book of distilled wisdom about grief (with few words) was a lot more challenging than the kind of writing I am used to. My book has benefited greatly from the thriving community spirit of this publishing house. Each department has been enjoyable to work with and well prepared for each stage of publication.

I am profoundly grateful to my clients who have trusted me as their guide in grief. I am in awe of their courage as they dive into their depths, embrace their grief, and transform their lives. They are the inspiration for this book—to participate so intimately with them in this process of healing is truly a gift that nourishes my soul.

Special thanks to my students at John F. Kennedy University, who over the past eleven years have shared themselves so generously in our classes—and who provided me with an ongoing laboratory for refining, adjusting, deepening, and expanding my strategies for grieving effectively without feeling overwhelmed.

A deep bow to my beloved teacher Stephen Levine. For several years in the seventies I had the immense good fortune to meditate weekly with him and attend his first workshops on death, dying, and grieving. My practice since has been to humbly integrate those teachings into every aspect of my life—and into every page of this book. This book is blessed by the wise, compassionate words of his foreword.

A joyous song of gratitude to my family and friends (whose names are written in my heart), who sustain, inspire, and encourage me in my creative process as we travel through life together—you've helped me in more ways than you can imagine. In dedicating this book to my son, I celebrate his big heart, creative spirit, and enormous capacity for compassion. Shine on, Taylor! My husband, Jon, offers the best insights and criticism of anyone I know—balanced exquisitely with his tender love, support, and authentic presence. I am blessed beyond measure to have enjoyed forty-three years of marriage to this extraordinary man. My enduring love and deepest gratitude to him.

Photograph by Paul Schraub

Alexandra Kennedy, MA, LMFT, is a psychotherapist in private practice thirty-nine years and author of *Losing a Parent*; *The Infinite Thread: Healing Relationships Beyond Loss*; and *How Did I Miss All This Before? Waking Up to the Magic of Our Ordinary Lives*. She is an adjunct faculty member of John F. Kennedy University and has taught at the University of California Santa Cruz Extension and the Institute of Transpersonal Psychology. She has been interviewed in *USA Today*, the *San Jose Mercury News*, the *San Francisco Examiner*, and the *Boston Herald*, as well as on NPR's *Talk of the Nation*, CNN's *Sonja Live*, and on KQED's *Family Talk* and *New Dimensions Radio*.

Foreword writer **Stephen Levine** is an American poet, author, and teacher, who along with his wife and spiritual partner Ondrea Levine, is best known for his work on death and dying. He is the author of *Who Dies, Healing into Life and Death, Turning Toward the Mystery, Becoming Kuan Yin*, and many other books.

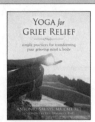

Also available from
Alexandra Kennedy

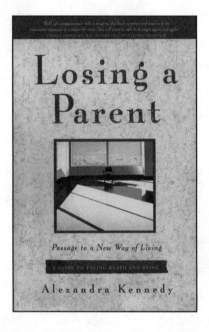

HarperOne
An Imprint of HarperCollins*Publishers*